The 25
SCARIEST PLACES
in the World

Written by Phyllis Emert
Illustrations by Lauren Jarrett

Lowell House
Juvenile
Los Angeles

CONTEMPORARY BOOKS
Chicago

Cover illustration by Ted Fuka

Publisher: Jack Artenstein
Vice President/General Manager, Juvenile Division: Elizabeth Amos
Director of Publishing Services: Rena Copperman
Editorial Director: Brenda Pope-Ostrow
Project Editor: Michael Artenstein
Managing Editor, Juvenile Division: Jessica Oifer
Art Director: Lisa-Theresa Lenthall
Production/Typesetting: Laurie Young

Library of Congress Catalog Card Number: 95-494

ISBN: 1-56565-277-0

Manufactured in the United States of America

10 9 8 7 6 5 4 3 2 1

Lowell House books can be purchased at special discounts when ordered in bulk for premiums and special sales. Contact Department JH at the following address:

Lowell House Juvenile
2029 Century Park East
Suite 3290
Los Angeles, CA 90067

Contents

FOR TWYLA WARDELL

SPECIAL THANKS to the following for their help and cooperation in writing this book: Dale Kaczmarek, President of the Ghost Research Society (P. O. Box 205, Oak Lawn, Il 60454-0205); Waymon Benifield of the Alabama Department of Transportation; Department of Parks and Recreation—City and County of Denver; Niagara Frontier State Park and Recreation Commission; George Burgess, Director of the International Shark Attack File—American Elasmobranch Society; and last but not least, my talented editor, Michael "Pappy" Artenstein.

Introduction

You are holding in your hand a guide to the scariest places on earth . . . a virtual potpourri of fear . . . a sourcebook of worldwide locations guaranteed to stimulate your imagination, if not frighten you senseless.

There are varying degrees of scariness, and this book covers them all, from heart-stopping terror to creepy uneasiness to run-for-your-life danger!

It's fascinating, fast-paced, and frightening, but never, never boring.

A word of warning: Do not read this book when you're all alone . . . especially at night!

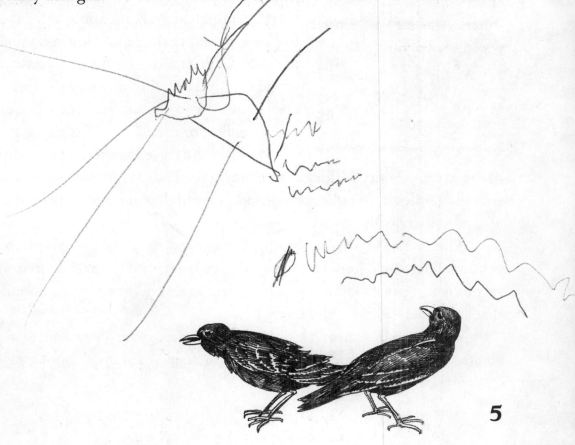

El Panteón Cemetery Guanajuato, Mexico

"**H**ere it is!" the man exclaimed, stabbing a finger in his guide-book. "El Panteón Cemetery, and it's less than a mile from here."

"Great!" said the man's wife. "We can see the mummies before it gets dark."

The young American couple left the café and began walking down the street under the dying Mexican sunlight. Chatting as they went, their arms interlocked, they were utterly oblivious to the gruesome, terrifying display they were about to encounter.

Every year thousands of thrill seekers make their way through the catacombs, or underground passages, at El Panteón Cemetery in

GUANAJUATO, MEXICO

Guanajuato, Mexico. For a nominal fee they can view the more than one hundred mummies on display there—bodies that were originally buried in the cemetery directly above but were exhumed from their graves when families or friends could no longer afford to pay for grave maintenance. Because of the extremely dry Mexican climate and the high amount of salt in the soil, the bodies have not decomposed. Instead they have been preserved in all their otherworldy horror.

The mummies of Guanajuato have existed since before the turn of the century. Back then, however, it would have been hard to imagine that so revolting a scene would one day become a macabre tourist attraction. But that's precisely what has happened.

When you descend the stairway to the catacombs, you come to a vaulted corridor where the mummies (which, incidentally, are not wrapped in gauze like the ones in the movies) are on display. There, you are free to examine their withered remains up close—if you have the stomach for it. In the well-lighted corridor you will see the mummies standing or sitting in dreadful silence behind their individual glass coffins. Some of them reach out with open arms as if pleading. Others appear to be struggling, as though they were trying to break out of their confinement.

But it's the faces of the mummies which, once seen, become imprinted in people's minds forever. The awful, empty eyesockets seem to stare directly at you. The skeletal mouths hang open in silent but eternal screams, revealing long incisors that look more like fangs than human teeth. Some of the mummies wear shoes and have facial hair, with remnants of burial clothes draped over their parched and withering remains.

One thing is certain: No one—not even the most die-hard horror buff—can be too prepared for what awaits them in the catacombs beneath El Panteón Cemetery.

Every year thousands of thrill seekers pay to view the gruesome mummies on display in the catacombs beneath El Panteón Cemetery.

Komodo Island
Lesser Sundas, Indonesia

The huge creature has an armor-plated head and large, razor-sharp claws. Its thick, forked tongue flickers in and out of its open mouth. The massive body, with its short, thick tail, is more than ten feet long and weighs over two hundred pounds.

The creature is a Komodo dragon, the world's largest monitor lizard, so called because they supposedly warn crocodiles of the approach of man. Several thousand of them wander freely on Komodo Island as well as parts of the Indonesian islands Rintja, Padar, and Flores.

These isolated islands provide an ideal habitat for the Komodo dragon, consisting of monsoon forests and savannah grasslands where game is plentiful. They feed on the dead and rotted flesh of goats, wild pigs, water buffalo, rusa deer, and feral horses. The giant lizard has even been known to feed on human corpses if given the opportunity.

Although it is believed that Komodo dragons reaching twenty feet or more in length do exist on the island, the largest that have actually been observed are about ten feet long. These large lizards are very dangerous and will attack and eat any smaller creatures they can corner. The large monitors are not very fast, and most humans can outrun them. Some people, however, have not been so fortunate.

According to a 1972 article by Walter Auffenberg in the magazine *Natural History,* "People have been bitten in the shoulder or neck as they slept on the ground during the daytime. Others were attacked from behind while working in the bush." One person died in an unprovoked attack by a Komodo dragon, while another succumbed to a bacterial infection of bite wounds inflicted by the large lizard.

Auffenberg found that most of the huge monitor lizards avoided contact with humans, but some were very aggressive, entering tents and shelters and attacking people. Needless to say, residents of the island are always on the alert for these giant creatures!

Who said dinosaurs are extinct? On Komodo Island, the past merges with the present in the form of these remarkable, dangerous, and frightening creatures.

It is believed that some Komodo dragons reach twenty feet or more in length.

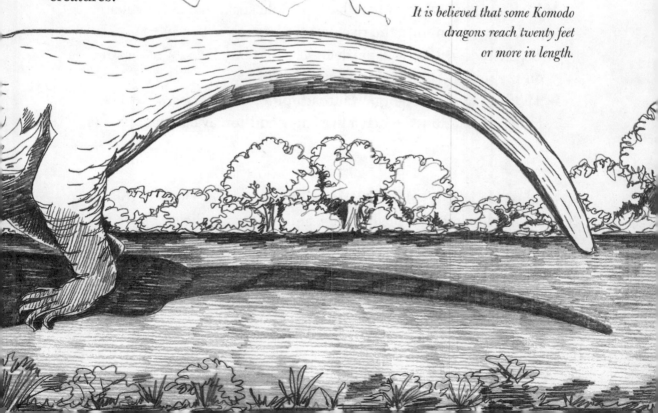

Devil's Hole
Niagara Gorge, New York

- June 28, 1854—A five-year-old girl falls 150 feet to her death near the cave known as Devil's Hole.
- September 6, 1901—President William McKinley rides the Great Gorge Railroad past Devil's Hole and hours later is hit by an assassin's bullet. He dies eight days later.
- March 12, 1907—Just past Devil's Hole, a sheet of ice crushes a railroad conductor to death. He had stepped out of his train to throw a switch on the tracks.
- February 27, 1913—The body of a sixty-five-year-old man is found fifty feet below the cliff at Devil's Hole.
- July 1, 1917—A railroad car near Devil's Hole derails and plunges into the river below, killing fourteen and injuring twenty-eight.
- June 7, 1929—A train near Devil's Hole strikes an elderly man and knocks him into the river, where he is swept away.
- September 5, 1932—A fourteen-year-old boy falls to his death on the railroad tracks near Devil's Hole.
- 1935—The Great Gorge Railroad route, which passes Devil's Hole, is abandoned when a five-thousand-ton avalanche uproots the tracks.

Author Dwight Whalen investigated the history of Devil's Hole cave and documented the bad luck and misfortune listed above in an article in *Fate* magazine in June 1992. Whalen discovered that over the years the cave and nearby area have seen more than their share of violent incidents that resulted in death, destruction, and injury.

Devil's Hole cave extends approximately twenty feet deep into the rock, about three miles below Niagara Falls and high above the whirling waters of Devil's Hole Rapids in the Niagara Gorge. A large boulder called Ambush Rock stands in front of the cave opening and was once thought to have completely covered the entrance.

NIAGARA GORGE, NEW YORK

Stories about the cave originated hundreds of years ago when ancient Seneca Indians in the Niagara region believed the cave to be the home of the devil. They called it the "abode of the Evil Spirit" and avoided the area so as not to disturb the demon within.

The Indians warned French explorer Robert La Salle not to enter the cave in 1669, but he wandered inside to investigate anyway. According to E. T. Williams' *History of Niagara County,* "His many misfortunes thereafter and his assassination later in Texas were attributed by the Senecas to the evil spirit he had antagonized by invading its domain."

On September 14, 1763, a convoy of British soldiers was attacked and massacred by Indians as it was passing Devil's Hole. Most of the nearly one hundred men were killed and then scalped. Some jumped to their death over the cliff to avoid the Indians. Only three survived the attack.

The awful noises of the massacre were heard by soldiers lower down in the gorge, and two companies came to the convoy's aid. These soldiers were also ambushed by the Indians and nearly all were killed. Although accounts differ, it is believed that nearly two hundred men were murdered that day near Devil's Hole.

It is said that the stream that runs through the ravine near the cave ran red with the blood of the victims of the Indians and is called Bloody Run even today. For many years after the Devil's Hole Massacre, remains such as human bones, pieces of wagons, and parts of guns were found strewn among the rocks in the gorge below the cave.

11

Whalen noted accidents and mishaps associated with Devil's Hole over the past fifty years. In 1949 a woman fell off the cliff but survived to tell the tale. In 1971 a man fell and broke his ankle. In 1982 two young men were attacked and injured by unknown assailants. That same year a fifteen-foot boulder crashed down into the gorge, narrowly missing a twenty-five-year-old man. In 1984 another man fell and was hospitalized with head and chest injuries. In 1987 two men in separate incidents were drowned in the river below Devil's Hole. No one knows how many additional cases were overlooked or not reported throughout the years.

Why are there so many accidents and tragedies associated with this gloomy, dark cave? Are the Indian legends true? Is Devil's Hole the home of an evil spirit or demon? Is there a curse on some of those who enter or venture nearby? Do deaths or injuries appease the demon for a number of years until the next incident?

Some say that the winding pathways and rocky cliffs make Devil's Hole the dangerous spot that it is. They say that accidents can and do happen—and they seem to occur very often at Devil's Hole!

There are others who wonder whether those who mysteriously lost their footing near the cave or were involved in accidents or mishaps were really controlled or affected by certain supernatural forces. Is it a curse or just a string of coincidences? Is it an evil spirit or just careless accidents?

Care to find out for yourself? Don't forget to bring your rabbit's foot!

Berry Pomeroy Castle Devon, England

In the late nineteenth century the famous English physician Sir Walter Farquhar visited the seriously ill wife of the steward (manager) of Berry Pomeroy Castle for the second day in a row. Worried about her condition, Sir Walter was both surprised and pleased to see that his patient was much improved.

After some conversation with the steward, the doctor mentioned a lovely stranger he saw the previous day while waiting to examine his patient. "I was sitting in the oak-paneled room with the loft when the door opened and in walked a remarkably beautiful young woman dressed in white," Sir Walter related. "She was wringing her hands and obviously very upset, then she glanced at me and disappeared up the stairs."

After hearing these words, the steward turned pale and began to pace the floor nervously.

DEVON, ENGLAND

"Are you all right? Did I say something wrong?" asked the concerned Sir Walter.

"What you saw was a ghost," the man replied in a murmur. "She was the daughter of a former owner of the castle."

"You're joking, of course," said Sir Walter. "Just who was she?"

"She's a ghost, all right. Little is known of her, but she was said to be as cruel and wicked as she was beautiful." The anguished steward sat down and placed his head in his hands. "Her appearance always is followed by the death of someone connected to the castle." Then the steward began to sob. "My wife, my wife."

"Get a hold of yourself," Sir Walter exclaimed. "You surely don't

An appearance by the ghostly lady in white
was once said to foreshadow the death of
someone connected to the castle.

believe that! Your wife is much better today and soon she'll be up and about."

The man shook his head. "The ghost was last seen here before my son drowned in an accident."

"Just a coincidence," Sir Walter replied. "You'll see. Your wife has improved remarkably."

Several hours later the steward's wife died suddenly and mysteriously, just as her husband had feared.

Shaken by the sudden turn of events, Sir Walter Farquhar was now convinced he had seen the ghost of the beautiful woman in white and wrote about his encounter in his published memoirs.

Feelings of intense dread, loneliness, and evil are how some visitors describe their experiences at the ruins of Berry Pomeroy Castle. Reports of hauntings can be traced back hundreds of years to the de la Pomerai family, who resided in the castle from 1066 to 1548. After it was sold, the new owners, the Seymours, built a large mansion within the castle walls, which was abandoned in the middle seventeenth century due to damage from the English Civil War. Further deterioration occurred in the early eighteenth century from a fire.

In addition to the ghost of the evil woman in white, visitors over the last fifty years have seen two other ghosts at the castle. Margaret de Pomeroy is said to walk the castle's ramparts in flowing white robes, calling on those she sees to come join her. Apparently Margaret was imprisoned in the castle dungeon and was starved to death by her sister Eleanor de Pomeroy. Both Eleanor and Margaret loved the same man, and Eleanor was jealous of her beautiful sister.

Consider for a moment the cruel and evil history of Pomeroy Castle. Is it any wonder that visitors leave the grounds with strong feelings of dread and terror?

Salem, Massachusetts

Descending the steps of the Witch Dungeon Museum in Salem, Massachusetts, the words *creepy* and *scary* immediately come to mind. It's dark, damp, and cold here, probably just the way it was more than three hundred years ago during the famous Salem witchcraft trials.

In 1692 a group of impressionable teenage girls claimed they had been bewitched by various members of the community. The girls exhibited bizarre behavior: barking, screaming, choking, and hysteria. They accused many of the older and respected Salem women of witchcraft, claiming to have seen them meeting with the devil.

The only evidence against the accused was what the magistrates called "spectral evidence," which basically meant anything that the girls said. If they said you met with the devil, whether you denied it or not,

SALEM, MASSACHUSETTS

you were guilty. The accused women were subsequently subjected to a body search for the devil's mark. Often a common birthmark or mole was considered proof of witchcraft.

If a woman was lucky enough to have a body free of blemishes, she was brought to court to confront the girls, who screamed and convulsed in her presence. It was believed that touching a witch would make her powerless, so each girl was forced to touch the accused, and lo and behold, the girls suddenly calmed down and acted normally. The magistrates took this as additional spectral evidence.

Before the witchcraft hysteria ended, nineteen people had been hanged and numerous others were imprisoned. The hysterical girls held in their hands the power of life and death in Salem, but when they accused the governor's wife of being a witch, they had gone too far. The governor ordered the so-called witches to be freed and the trials ended.

Scene after scene of the witch trials is depicted in the Witch Dungeon

Museum. But it is the one of Giles Corey and the awful way he died that is both fascinating and repulsive to visitors. Author Robert Cahill in his book *Haunted Happenings* calls Corey's death "the most tragic and brutal murder in the name of justice ever performed in America and certainly the most terrible in New England."

Giles Corey was one of several men accused of being a witch. Corey kept silent during his trial, determined to show contempt for the girls. According to the law back then, a person could not be tried if he or she didn't enter a plea, but there was a penalty for remaining mute: being slowly crushed under weights until the accused either pleaded or died. Once the person pleaded one way or the other, he or she was imprisoned and their money and property confiscated by the sheriff.

On September 19, 1692, the eighty-year-old man was stripped, taken to an open field near the jail, and made to lie down in a pit. As depicted in the museum scene, a large piece of wood was laid across his chest. As more and more rocks were placed on the board, the sheriff cried "Confess" over and over again. The weight increased and Corey's eyes and tongue bulged out of his face, but still the old man kept silent. Just before he died, Giles Corey supposedly called out, "I curse you and Salem!"

Many believe that the ghost of Giles Corey haunts the old burial ground near the jail in Salem where he died. An increase in sightings of Corey's ghost has also been noted right before a major disaster or setback to the town. The most famous was the Great Fire of 1914, which destroyed one-third of the city.

Just a coincidence? Possibly, but it's best not to stand too long in front of the scene of Giles Corey's death at the Witch Dungeon Museum. That feeling of a cold, spindly hand on your shoulder may not be just a figment of your imagination.

The East Coast of Australia off New South Wales and Queensland

The two honeymooners were scuba diving in Byron Bay, a popular beach area 370 miles north of Sydney, the capital of the Australian state of New South Wales. Married less than three weeks, Debbie and John Ford swam in beautiful clear water at a depth of about forty feet on June 9, 1993.

Suddenly John saw a huge, menacing shadow gliding beneath the surface of the water and heading toward his wife. John knew his wife was in great danger, so he swam between her and the advancing creature. Seconds later a sixteen-foot great white shark grabbed John in its huge jaws and began shaking him violently before taking him below the surface to his death. Debbie's life, however, had been spared.

Only four days earlier a thirty-four-year-old woman was attacked in another area off the eastern Australian coast and carried away by a twelve-foot great white shark. The attack was witnessed by her husband and five young children. The only remains recovered was a severed human leg with a diving fin still attached.

The east coast of Australia has had more shark attacks and fatalities than any part of the world, yet compared to other causes of death—like traffic accidents or disease—the risk to swimmers and scuba divers is still very minimal. Keep repeating that over and over again while you're splashing around in the waters off eastern Australian beaches!

The east coast of Australia has had more shark attacks than any other part of the world.

18

George Burgess, director of the International Shark Attack File, which keeps records of all reported shark attacks, wrote that "worldwide there are probably fifty to seventy-five shark attacks annually, resulting in about five to ten deaths." He declared that "many more people are injured and killed on land while driving to and from the beach than by sharks in the water."

The risk may be minimal, but that doesn't make the prospect of a shark attack any less unnerving. Great white sharks can grow to twenty-five or more feet in length and weigh several thousand pounds. Their terrifying

QUEENSLAND,
NEW SOUTH WALES,
AUSTRALIA

mouths, lined from front to back with razor-sharp teeth, are huge enough to swallow a person whole. These sharks are eating machines and will devour almost anything, including each other.

If the hairs on your neck aren't standing straight up from the very possibility of a shark attack, keep your eyes peeled for the beautiful but lethal Australian sea wasp, the most venomous jellyfish in the world. There are signs on certain eastern Australian beaches that read, "Warning—Sea Wasps Are Deadly in These Waters Between October and May."

Brush up against the transparent tentacles of the sea wasp and you'll experience terrible pain, partial paralysis, massive welts on the skin, and possible death within a few minutes. This lovely little creature has caused the deaths of sixty-six people off Queensland since 1880. Numerous others have survived the ordeal, often with lasting scars and very bad memories.

Regardless of the risks that may exist, more people than ever flock to the picturesque beaches of Australia's eastern coast for a day of fun in the sun and surf. After all, the odds are definitely in their favor.

Care to take a dip?

The Tomb of Tutankhamen Valley of the Kings, near Luxor, Egypt

"Death comes on wings to he who enters the tomb of a pharaoh."

Some say archaeologist Howard Carter found this warning on a tablet of hieroglyphics in the outer chamber of the tomb of the pharaoh Tutankhamen, which he discovered in 1923. Supposedly Carter took the tablet away before his workers could see the warning and become alarmed.

Others say it comes from a letter to the London *Times* written by novelist Marie Corelli in March of 1923. She quoted this phrase from an ancient Arabic book and predicted the death of those working in the tomb. Few in the press took note of her prophecy.

Several days after the letter appeared Lord Carnarvon, Carter's long-time financial sponsor, died unexpectedly of an infected insect bite that turned into pneumonia. Commenting on Carnarvon's death, Sir Arthur Conan Doyle, author and creator of Sherlock Holmes, said he believed that the death resulted from the pharaoh's revenge. From then on the "curse of Tutankhamen" made front page news.

Archaeologist Howard Carter's amazing discovery occurred six hundred miles up the river Nile near the town of Luxor in the Valley of the Kings. Here, more than three thousand years ago, the pharaohs of ancient Egypt were buried in magnificent hidden tombs.

Carter's find was considered the archaeological event of the century. First his workers unearthed a steep cut in the rock and then the upper edges of a stairway. Even today, descending the sixteen steps that lead into an underground passage ten feet high and six feet wide, and then through doorways into chamber after chamber, one feels as if the past and present have merged together. It's a strange and frightening feeling.

"For the moment, time as a factor in human life . . . lost its meaning," wrote Carter. "Three thousand, four thousand years . . . have passed and gone. . . . The very air you breathe, unchanged throughout the centuries, you share with those who laid the mummy to its rest. . . . You feel an intruder. . . ."

When Carter and Lord Carnarvon entered the pharaoh's outer rooms and burial chamber, they came upon riches and treasure beyond imagination—golden couches, statues, gold- and jewel-covered chariots, all stored within the pharaoh's tomb to help him complete his afterlife journey into paradise.

The mummy itself was placed in three coffins, one inside the other. The two outer coffins were made of wood and covered with gold and jewels. The inner coffin was made of solid gold and weighed nearly three thousand pounds, requiring four men to lift it. The twenty-one-inch solid gold funeral mask covering the mummy's face was an exact likeness of the seventeen-year-old boy-king.

But Lord Carnarvon hardly had a chance to share in these fabulous discoveries. He died suddenly at the age of fifty-seven. One newspaper wrote that Carnarvon cut his finger on a poisonous object in the tomb. Another reported that at the exact moment of his death (2:00 A.M.) at the Continental Hotel in Cairo, the whole city was immersed in the blackness of a power failure. Some said it was just a coincidence, that Cairo was often subject to blackouts. Meanwhile, at his home in England, Carnarvon's dog reportedly began to bark and howl at the moment of his passing, and the dog itself died soon after. Was it the curse or just another coincidence?

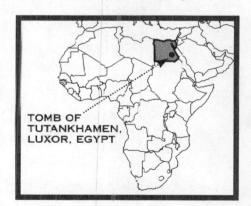

TOMB OF TUTANKHAMEN, LUXOR, EGYPT

According to the *Atlas of the Supernatural* by Derek and Julia Parker, an American archaeologist, an American financier, a British industrialist, and the radiologist who x-rayed the body of Tutankhamen all died mysteriously after visiting the tomb. Within seven years, twenty-two people connected with the tomb's discovery were dead.

Yet Howard Carter lived until 1939 when he died at the age of sixty-six, and Dr. Douglas Derry, who dissected the pharaoh's mummy, lived to be over eighty! One theory states that a type of airborne bacteria or virus purposely placed in the tomb by ancient Egyptians may have affected some people and not others, since most of those who died exhibited symptoms of depression, numbness, and lethargy. Were Carter and Derry immune to the curse? Perhaps.

In the 1960s the treasures of the tomb of Tutankhamen were placed in a traveling exhibit that visited major cities throughout the world. The tour was coordinated by the director-general of the Antiquities Department of the Cairo Museum, where the valuable collection is usually displayed. The fifty-two-year-old director-general, Gemal Mehrez, told one reporter, "I've been involved with tombs and mummies of pharaohs all my life. I'm living proof that it was all coincidence!"

A month later Mehrez was dead.

Bracken Cave
near San Antonio, Texas

"What is that?" the man said, pointing to a dark mass in the distance. It was an early August evening in central Texas.

"It almost looks like a tornado funnel," said his wife, "but that's impossible. The weather here is calm and beautiful. There's not a cloud in the sky."

The man studied the shadowy formation. "I've never seen a funnel like that before, swirling around so high. It's almost as if it were . . ."

"Alive," whispered the woman quietly.

The man turned to look at his wife and saw fear, as well as wonder and curiosity, in her face.

"Swarms of birds?" the man asked with a frown on his face.

"Bats!" cried his wife. "I remember reading about it in the guidebook. They're bats emerging from their cave to find food!"

The man shuddered. *Millions of bats,* he repeated to himself, then shot a quick glance at his wife. "Let's get back to San Antonio."

Beginning in the spring more than twenty million Mexican free-tailed bats emerge daily from Bracken Cave before sundown. Located less than twenty miles from downtown San Antonio, this huge cave is home to the largest bat colony in the world.

The huge flocks of bats climb as high as eleven thousand feet to catch tailwinds that carry them long distances at speeds of more than sixty miles per hour. In one single night's feeding these bats eat three to four billion insects. One bat alone can catch five hundred mosquito-sized insects in sixty minutes!

The colony from Bracken Cave consumes about two hundred and fifty tons of insects each and every night, so it's not surprising that the city and suburbs of San Antonio depend upon the bats for insect control. Their nightly trips for food lessen the need for chemical pesticides in the entire central Texas region.

During the day the roof of Bracken Cave is completely covered with 240 tons of resting bats that are hanging upside down. They produce enormous amounts of droppings, which accumulate on the cave floor to become what is known as guano. This rich layer of fertilizer is covered with millions of carnivorous beetles. If a young bat learning to fly makes an unexpected landing on the cave floor, the beetles can reduce it to bones within minutes.

Emergency landings seldom occur, since the bat maneuvers in the dark by the use of ultrasonic vibrations (called *echolocation*). These signals generate echoes in the form of high frequency sounds that enable the bat to be guided at night and to detect prey. In total darkness a bat can detect objects as fine as a human hair.

Just the thought of so many bats together in one place may make some people weak in the knees. Yet these creatures are harmless to man. Of the nearly one thousand types of bats in existence, only the vampire bats of Mexico and Central and South America are capable of passing diseases on to animals and occasionally man, and only a very small portion actually do so.

Bracken Cave is owned and protected by Bat Conservation International (BCI). The cave is not accessible to the public at the present time, but

the incredible scene of the bats leaving the cave before
sundown each day is visible many miles away.

For some it's a frightening and creepy sight,
even a haunting experience. If you can manage
to control the shudder of fear, it's a vision
you'll never forget.

*Bracken Cave is home to the
largest bat colony in the world.*

Csejthe Castle Carpathian Mountains, Hungary

Are those dark spots on the castle walls bloodstains? Or are they just blackened soot from the destructive fire caused by lightning in the eighteenth century? Is your feeling of dread and foreboding all in your mind?

You don't have to be psychic to pick up the loathsome vibrations at Csejthe Castle. The ruins of this once massive, horror-filled fortress in the foothills of the Carpathian Mountains in Central Europe still stand today. High on the hilltop overlooking the village of Csejthe, the castle was once the home of Countess Elizabeth Báthory.

Often called the Vampire Lady or the Blood Countess, Báthory was responsible for the murders of an astonishing 650 young women in the late sixteenth and early seventeenth centuries. If craving blood is the primary distinctive characteristic of a vampire, then Elizabeth Báthory had to be the most notorious human vampire in history.

Báthory was a wealthy and beautiful woman from one of Europe's great aristocratic families. She was a devoted wife to Count Ferencz Nadasdy and a loving mother to her four children. But she had two unusual and bizarre obsessions: Báthory was preoccupied with maintaining her beauty and youthful appearance, and she took pleasure in inflicting pain on people.

With the death of her husband in 1604, Báthory's obsessions quickly degenerated into complete madness. She began to believe that bathing in and drinking the blood of young, attractive girls would help to maintain her beauty. Indulging her gruesome habits on a daily basis required a steady stream of unsuspecting young girls. Most were lured to the castle under false pretenses. Few were ever seen alive again.

Disposing of the victims' bodies was a time-consuming and difficult task for Báthory's servants. Most were buried in nearby fields, but some were found by the villagers, who attributed the murders to vampires.

Over the years the unexplained disappearances and body count mounted, and the villagers began to talk. The Báthorys were powerful nobles, but it was hard for the people to ignore the screams coming from the castle night after night. Finally they banded together and denounced the countess to the king.

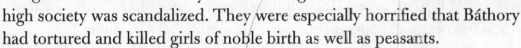

In 1611 an investigation of the murders led straight to Elizabeth Báthory. Austro-Hungarian high society was scandalized. They were especially horrified that Báthory had tortured and killed girls of noble birth as well as peasants.

Her servant accomplices were all tried and executed, but the countess' life was spared in order to avoid further disgrace to the illustrious Báthory and Nadasdy families. She was sentenced to imprisonment at Csejthe Castle for the rest of her life.

The king instructed workmen to wall up the windows and doors to Báthory's small room. Only an opening for food connected her to the outside world. A gallows was built at each of the four corners of the castle as a sign that justice had been done.

Elizabeth Báthory died alone after three and a half years in her tiny prison. Some believe her spirit lingers on, yearning for just one more bath of blood.

It's best not to stay too long in the ruins of Csejthe Castle, especially at dusk when the last light slips away. You just might see something that will haunt you for the rest of your life.

Old House Woods near Mathews Courthouse, Virginia

It stands now as it has stood for hundreds of years: a dark and gloomy pine forest quietly guarding its secrets from intruders. Located about four miles from the town of Mathews Courthouse, Virginia, the woods are less than a quarter mile from Chesapeake Bay.

"Old House Woods is haunted. I would advise you to stay away from there," declared local merchant Jesse V. Hudgins in 1926. "Probably there's gold buried there—lots of it. But for all I care, or anybody else that lives in the neighborhood, it can remain until the crack of doom."

Hudgins first confronted a ghostly resident of Old House Woods late one October night when he was seventeen years old. He was driving a wagon into town to get the doctor for a sick neighbor. As he neared the

MATHEWS COURTHOUSE, VIRGINIA

vacant and broken-down building known as the Old House, which stands by the side of the road and is surrounded by towering pines, he noticed a strange light in the woods moving in the same direction he was going.

"My horse, usually afraid of nothing, cowered and trembled violently," he explained. As Hudgins pulled even with the light, he saw a large man wearing a suit of armor and carrying a musket. What disturbed Hudgins was that the man was moving without making a sound, as if he were floating along the road instead of walking on it.

"My horse stopped dead still," recalled Hudgins.

When the figure stopped to face him, Hudgins stared back at the man and noticed that the woods behind him "became alive with lights and moving forms." Some of the figures carried guns or shovels while others dug near one of the trees.

"As my gaze returned to the first shadowy figure, what I saw was not the man in armor but a skeleton, and every bone of it was visible through the iron armor as if it were made of glass," Hudgins recalled. "The skull grinned at me horribly. Then, raising aloft a sword, which I had not . . . noticed, the awful specter started toward me menacingly."

Hudgins' terror was so great he felt his mind give way to unconsciousness. The next thing he knew he awoke in his bed surrounded by family members who told him he had been found on the road beyond Old House Woods. The horse, to the day it died, trembled and cowered whenever it approached the woods.

Some residents attribute the ghastly appearances to a band of pirates who used the woods to hide their booty but died in a dispute over how to divide the spoils.

A man named Harry Forrest, who lived six hundred feet from Old House Woods, saw and heard many strange things over the years: armies of marching British redcoats; moving lights and the sounds of digging; and a strange woman in white, whose appearance always signaled an upcoming storm.

There have been several attempts to dig for the buried treasure that most agree is hidden in Old House Woods, but all have resulted in tragedy or failure. One man disappeared; another was killed by lightning. The daughter of still another died mysteriously and suddenly.

It stands now as it will probably stand for another hundred years— dark, foreboding, and frightening, guarding its many secrets from intruders. Whoever walks in Old House Woods does so at his or her own risk.

The Tower of London
London, England

Terrified screams, headless ghosts, phantom figures, disappearing apparitions, floating heads—it's all routine at the Tower of London, historically one of the bloodiest spots in the world. In fact, the Tower is the oldest occupied building on earth today—older than the Vatican in Rome, the Louvre in Paris, and the Kremlin in Moscow.

LONDON, ENGLAND

The tower was used as a prison, complete with torture chamber and a place of execution, and hundreds of people were hanged or beheaded there. Their ghosts still frighten visitors and haunt the Tower grounds today.

The ghost most often seen by tourists and guards is that of Anne Boleyn, the second wife of King Henry VIII. Anne was beheaded in 1536 after she was found guilty of being unfaithful to the king. The real reason for her execution was that she couldn't bear Henry a son and heir to the throne. There was no such thing as a recognized divorce, and the king wanted to be free to take a new wife. Anne left her legacy in her daughter, Elizabeth I, who later became queen of England and reigned for forty-five years!

A small, pretty woman, Anne was terrified of being beheaded by an ax. Occasionally more than one blow was necessary to sever the head from the body, and it wasn't a particularly pleasant experience for the victim, the executioner, or the spectators. So she asked the king to allow her a quick death with a sword. The king agreed, and a Frenchman was brought over from Calais, a city in France, to perform the act.

On May 19, Anne was helped up the steps of the scaffold on the Tower grounds and knelt down in prayer. A bandage was placed over her eyes, and the executioner cut off her head with one sharp slice. Anne's ghost, with and without her head, has been seen alone or in a procession, usually close to the Bloody Tower, where she spent her last days.

One of the most horrible executions that occurred in the Tower of London was that of Margaret, the Countess of Salisbury, in 1541. The seventy-year-old noblewoman did not die with dignity. She was led screaming to the executioner's block, then escaped from the guards and ran around like a crazed maniac. The guards had to drag her back to the block and force her to bend down. Ax in hand, the executioner missed not once but *four* times, before the fifth blow finally severed her head from her body. Is it any wonder that Anne Boleyn wanted a skilled swordsman at her beheading? The countess Margaret's terrified screams are still heard near the site of her death on or near the anniversary of her execution.

There have always been ravens living on and around the grounds of the Tower of London. An old legend states that if the ravens leave, the Tower

Anne Boleyn, 2nd wife of Henry VIII, was beheaded in 1536, but her ghost—with or without her head— has been sighted frequently on the Tower grounds.

will fall and so will "the greatness and glory of Britain." Today six of these black birds have had their wings clipped so that they can't fly away.

Edgar Allan Poe once described ravens as "things of evil" and questioned whether they were birds or devils. It seems appropriate that these small, dark creatures inhabit a place that has seen so much horror.

Marfa, Texas

In 1883 Robert Ellison and several other cowboys were driving a herd of cattle across the desert area of Mitchell Flat between the small towns of Alpine and Marfa in southwestern Texas. They were camped for the night when Ellison noticed some peculiar balls of light at the base of the Chinati Mountains in the distance.

When he pointed them out to his companions, the men came up with a logical explanation. "They're just the lights from some Apache campfires," they explained.

But after watching them for a while, Ellison realized something scary and mysterious was happening. *Those are definitely not campfires,* he thought to himself. *Glowing balls of light . . . moving up and down and bouncing back and forth. What could possibly be doing that?*

The next morning Ellison and the others set out to find the Indian campfires and solve the mystery, but they found nothing at all. Speaking with others in the area, Ellison found that the local settlers had always seen strange lights flickering about and moving through the desert. But no one had any explanation as to what they were. Most people in the area just called them "ghost lights."

As the years passed and the lights near Marfa continued to appear, so did the sightings and the theories of explanation. Some researchers stated they were the headlights of cars reflected by the different temperature layers in the atmosphere. It sounds logical until you remember there were no car headlights when the lights were first sighted in the nineteenth century.

One scientist declared that the glowing balls of light were composed of electrically charged atomic particles. Others claimed they were a form of ball lightning, some type of electromagnetic energy, or even ionized gases escaping from faultlines in the earth. No theory has yet been proven to explain the strange and unusual lights.

Eyewitness accounts by those who have personally encountered the ghost lights make one wonder whether the supernatural rather than the scientific has something to do with this scary phenomenon.

One man traveling on Highway 90 west of Marfa saw the lights come up behind his truck and then disappear suddenly. Another man was frightened when a melon-sized ball of light stayed outside his car window for two miles no matter how fast he drove down the highway.

Two geologists documented their close encounters with the Marfa ghost lights in 1973. Pat Kenney and Elwood Wright observed the lights at a distance, swinging in an arc and turning completely around in a loop. "They appeared to be playing," said Kenney and Wright.

The two men wanted a closer look, so they drove onto Mitchell Flat along a dirt road toward the Chinati Mountains. Because of the full moon they drove without headlights for a while, then stopped and waited. Suddenly they saw two ghost lights about a thousand feet away moving no more than three or four feet above the ground.

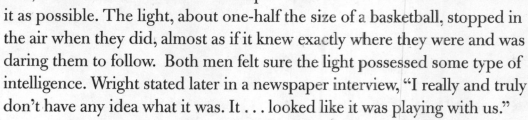

The second light seemed slower than the first, so the men decided to sneak up as close to it as possible. The light, about one-half the size of a basketball, stopped in the air when they did, almost as if it knew exactly where they were and was daring them to follow. Both men felt sure the light possessed some type of intelligence. Wright stated later in a newspaper interview, "I really and truly don't have any idea what it was. It . . . looked like it was playing with us."

Are they trying to communicate something to us? If the answer is yes, what are they trying to tell us, and what is significant about Marfa, Texas, and other spots in the world where strange lights have been observed?

There are many questions, and nobody has the answers. In the meantime the ghost lights of Marfa, Texas, continue to amaze people and defy all explanation.

Mariana Trench off Guam, Pacific Ocean

Sea monsters, giant squids, monstrous eels, grotesque fish? What strange creatures lurk in the dark, cold, high-pressure depths of the ocean floor? Man has barely begun to penetrate this last unexplored region on earth, which holds the promise of new discoveries and a wealth of knowledge.

The deepest part of the ocean, Challenger Deep in the Mariana Trench (a deep ditch or furrow) off the island of Guam, is 36,198 feet straight down. That's seven miles below the surface of the Pacific Ocean! Mount Everest, the highest mountain in the world, could fit into the Challenger Deep and still be more than a *mile* from the surface.

This deepest part of the ocean is called the abyss. It is blacker

than night all the time, since sunlight cannot penetrate water so deep. It is very cold—only a little above freezing—and the pressure is a crushing three and a half tons per square inch!

Do monstrous sea creatures of huge dimensions lurk in the abyss? Many scientists say no, but several believe they may indeed exist. Giant squids up to fifty-seven feet in length have already been found in the waters off New Zealand, and scientists believe there may be others that are even larger and more powerful. Giant squids of the Humboldt Current off Peru in South America are so ferocious and dangerous that they've been known to attack fishermen.

According to C. P. Idyll in his book *Abyss*, a type of eel larva six feet in length was discovered by a Danish research ship in the deep sea. "This suggests," wrote Idyll,

Do monstrous sea creatures lurk in the deepest part of the ocean?

"the existence of an enormous eel of sixty or seventy feet, a length that would surely qualify it as a sea monster."

Dr. Karl Shuker proposes the possibility of giant jellyfish whose stings are as deadly as those of the Australian sea wasp, another deadly denizen of the east Australian coast. "It is very possible that jellyfish notably larger than any yet recorded by science do exist in our world's vast oceans," declared Shuker. "Most may well exist in the abyssal depths, where man at present has scarcely begun to penetrate."

Only once has anyone ventured this deep. On January 23, 1960, Jacques Piccard and Lieutenant Donald Walsh of the United States Navy traveled to the bottom of the Mariana Trench in the bathyscaph *Trieste,* a specially designed diving apparatus.

The *Trieste* spent five hours descending into the Challenger Deep and only twenty minutes on the floor of the abyss. During that short time the men reported seeing nothing unusual.

The creatures that populate the ocean depths have adapted to the peculiar conditions in unusual ways. Most are quite bizarre in their appearance, yet small in their overall size. Gulpers are fish with huge mouths and small bodies. Hatchet fish also have large, gulping mouths and compressed bodies that are as thin as coins. Brotulids have big, grotesque heads that taper into long, pointed tails.

According to marine biologist Sylvia Earle, "It's still ironic that there are more footprints on the moon than there are on the bottom of the sea." Once the last great frontier of deep-ocean exploration is conquered, will scientists discover an abundance of new information to add to our knowledge of life on earth? Or will they encounter gigantic and threatening sea creatures and other monstrosities of nature? Only time will tell.

Hampton Court
Middlesex, England

Accompanied by two guards, the young woman with long, flowing hair suddenly broke loose from her captors and ran screaming through the gallery. Her husband, who was in the chapel hearing evening prayers, ignored his young wife's pleadings for mercy. The woman was recaptured and dragged away shrieking and sobbing by the guards, her screams strangely merging with the singing of the chapel choir.

The husband was King Henry VIII of England. The wife was Lady Catherine Howard, Henry's fifth spouse, who was eventually tried and found guilty of treason and beheaded in 1542. The incident occurred at Hampton Court, the beautiful palace by the river Thames where Henry often resided.

It's been more than 450 years since Lady Catherine's death. However, the tragic replay of her futile attempt to escape from King Henry's guards takes place nearly every year on or around the anniversary of the incident. Her ghost runs through what is now called "the Haunted Gallery" screaming and shrieking. Numerous witnesses have heard or seen her ghost.

MIDDLESEX, ENGLAND

Many other apparitions roam the grounds of Hampton Court including that of Henry's third wife, Jane Seymour. One of the few to keep her head, Jane Seymour died in 1537, only one week after bearing Henry his only son and heir, Prince Edward. Lady Jane's ghost, clad in white, wanders the halls carrying a lighted candle and often walks through doors and glides down staircases. Her ghost is responsible for many a servant handing in their resignation. Just imagine how unsettling it would be to see a specter of Lady Jane floating noiselessly toward you in a long, darkened corridor!

Then there's the story of the lady in gray, another ghostly resident. Princess Frederica of Hanover, a guest at Hampton Court, once came face to face with what she described as a "tall, gaunt figure dressed in a long gray robe, with a hood on her head and her lanky hands outstretched before her." Later the princess realized she had seen the ghost of Mrs. Sybil Penn, Prince Edward's nursemaid, who died there of smallpox in 1568.

In the nineteenth century a sealed room was discovered, which was believed to be Penn's. Her often-used spinning wheel was found inside. For years after the room was unsealed servants and guests at Hampton Court complained of cold hands on their faces, footsteps outside the door, loud crashing noises, strange lights, and voices at night.

Peter Underwood in *A Gazetteer of British Ghosts* relates an incident about two close female friends, one who was granted a residence at Hampton Court and the other who went to live in Germany. One night the Englishwoman saw a shadowy image of her friend, dressed entirely in black except for white gloves, climbing the staircase toward her. As the figure drew closer the Englishwoman fainted. Several days later the woman learned that her friend had died on the same day her ghost appeared at Hampton Court. Her friend had made an unusual request for her funeral. She wanted to be buried in black—with white gloves!

Hampton Court is rich in history with an underlying layer of violence and death. Only those with calm nerves should dare to visit this lively breeding ground of ghostly activities.

The Spy House
Port Monmouth,
New Jersey

The ghosts at the Spy House rattle appliances, make strange noises, push buttons, turn on radios, flip people's hair, move things around, and appear and disappear frequently. Some have even gone home with visitors they take a liking to.

This three-story wooden house, which was made into a museum in the late 1960s, is located on Sandy Hook Bay on the New Jersey coast. It is literally swarming with ghosts and other supernatural phenomena, whose frightening appearances have been witnessed often in broad daylight!

Arthur Myers in his book *A Ghosthunter's Guide* interviewed many people who experienced ghost sightings at the Spy House. One man described several children dressed in old-fashioned clothes playing near the house. "A girl ran through me," he said. "Then they were . . . gone."

A psychic named Gordon Banta recalled how he thought he had run over a little girl with his car, but when he left his vehicle to have a look around, he found no trace of her! The ghost suddenly appeared by his side and actually spoke to Banta. "She told me she lived in a house nearby . . . and had been run over by a horse and wagon."

The rich and varied history of the Spy House is thought to have contributed to the large number of spirits that are seen in and around the grounds. Barely a day goes by when a psychic does not visit the area to investigate.

The present building was put together from four smaller buildings that date back to the 1600s. One of these belonged to Thomas Whitlock, the first permanent white resident of New Jersey, who traded with the local Indians. Visions of brutal Indian attacks on the house were experienced by one visiting psychic who explained them as "energy imprints" from the past and not actual spirits.

During the Revolutionary War the house was used as an inn and tavern, often frequented by British Commander Lord Charles Cornwallis, whose ghost is often seen today. The inn was also used as a gathering place for American patriots who watched the movement of British ships in New York Harbor.

PORT MONMOUTH, NEW JERSEY

Pirates occupied the house in the early 1800s and are believed to have used it to hide stolen goods and even kill hostages. It is said that four tunnels exist behind the old stone walls in the cellar. Gertrude Neidlinger, who runs the museum in the Spy House, believes the tunnels may still contain hidden pirate treasure.

Jane Dougherty of the Society of Parapsychology of New Jersey gets bad vibrations from the Spy House cellar. It was "used for many purposes, some of them involving fear and distress . . . " she said. "It was a place that pirates put people before they killed them. It was an animal slaughter room. It's a terrible feeling down there."

Author Myers explored the locked cellar with Neidlinger. He felt nothing unusual there, but his tape recorder behaved very strangely. It stopped then started again and later played back the sound of distorted voices. Myers assumed they were his and Neidlinger's voices, but he wasn't sure. Strangely enough the recorder worked fine once they were back upstairs.

Additional ghosts sighted in or around the Spy House include original owner Thomas Whitlock, a sea captain's wife named Abigail, Captain Morgan (the pirate) and his first mate, a childless woman named Penelope, a boy named Peter, and other children of assorted ages.

There's no question that strange things frequently happen at the Spy House, whose richly checkered past evidently lives on in the present.

America's Stonehenge Mystery Hill, North Salem, New Hampshire

This four-thousand-year-old stone complex of enclosed chambers, huge slabs, and narrow passageways may be the oldest man-made site in all of North America. Yet no one knows for sure who built it, where these people came from, and what purpose the complex served.

The mysterious stone structures of America's Stonehenge are surrounded by the rolling hills, green trees, and thick-growing shrubs of New England. It's easy to let your imagination wander as you walk up the trail past double stone walls to the first structure, known as the Watchhouse. Located outside the main complex, you wonder whether the guards of a mysterious prehistoric people once watched for unwelcome intruders from this vantage point.

From here a double-walled path leads to the main complex of stone structures. They're all about five feet high with roofs made of six- to ten-ton slabs of rock. How could such heavy stones (monoliths), which are held together by their own weight and careful positioning, have been raised up so high?

Next you come to a giant four-and-one-half-ton grooved slab known as the sacrificial table, which is supported on four stone legs. It's not hard to imagine people in dark hooded robes who may have surrounded this altar of sacrifice. Perhaps a human or animal victim was laid out before them on the slab amidst the sounds of strange chants and incantations, then a sharpened object was held high above the victim's chest and . . .

Turning away, you notice the grooves cut into the slab, which most researchers agree carried the runoff of blood underneath the rock to a network of stone drains.

Near the sacrificial table is a covered passage that leads to the largest structure in the complex, the Oracle Chamber. It's twenty-two-and-one-half feet wide and six-and-one-half feet high. A tubelike shaft leads from

 the large chamber directly under the sacrificial slab. Speaking through this opening, a person's voice in the large chamber is amplified and easily heard at the altar.

The outside area contains large stone monoliths arranged in a circular pattern. Robert Stone, owner of America's Stonehenge, found that many of these monoliths have astronomical significance. Standing at the sacrificial table, Stone discovered that the sun rose and set directly over certain monoliths. Two stones aligned with the setting sun at the annual summer and winter solstices on June 21 and December 21, respectively. Others marked sunrises and sunsets on important days of ancient pre-Christian holidays.

Just who were these prehistoric people who practiced human and/or animal sacrifice yet had an advanced knowledge of construction and astronomy? There are many theories.

Researcher Jean Hunt proposed a theory of a superior civilization that existed thousands of years ago but died out completely, leaving no records behind. Perhaps, according to Hunt, knowledge of this civilization came to us in the form of myths and legends that dealt with powerful magicians, wizards, or elves. Did such beings really once exist in the past, but are now preserved only in children's stories?

Scientists as well as psychics who have studied the site disagree on whether the people who built America's Stonehenge were native to North America or once came from ancient Europe. One theory states that a small group of people from prehistoric Europe migrated here so they could practice their beliefs of blood sacrifice freely and without persecution. Another theory holds that an ancient but highly intelligent race of people were wiped out in some type of massive disaster that destroyed their civilization, leaving behind only the ruins in New Hampshire.

America's Stonehenge is a scary and mysterious place that is totally enveloped by the past. Standing among the stone chambers and monoliths, it's easy to understand how certain psychic or sensitive individuals could pick up strong vibrations from a previous era. Perhaps someday the puzzle will be solved. In the meantime the research and study continue and the mystery remains.

Just who built the mysterious stone structures known as America's Stonehenge?

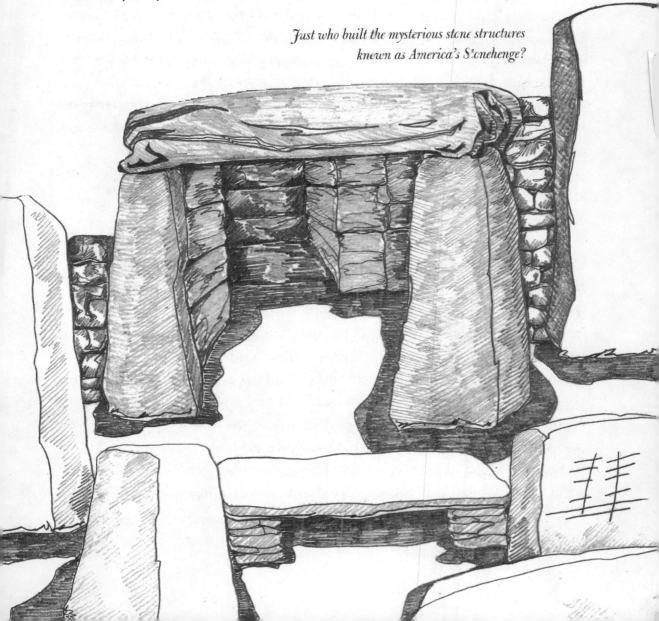

Glamis Castle
Glamis, Angus, Scotland

It doesn't matter whether you visit Glamis Castle on a dark and stormy night or in the bright sunlight of a summer's day. You can't help but feel that this impressive and huge structure is a very scary, strange, and mysterious place.

Built in the fourteenth century, Glamis is the oldest inhabited castle in Scotland and is home to frequently sighted ghosts and spirits. The castle was originally the residence of the lords of Glamis, who lost their family fortune, after which the castle passed into the hands of Patrick Lyons in the mid-seventeenth century. Lyons renovated the place, built up the fortune, and was made the Earl of Strathmore.

ANGUS, SCOTLAND

According to legend, in the early nineteenth century the first son of the eleventh Earl of Strathmore was born terribly deformed. The child had a large, hairy egg-shaped body with no neck and tiny arms and legs. A special hidden room was built for him in the depths of the castle, and his existence was kept secret because of his horrible appearance.

The Monster of Glamis, as he came to be known, was the true heir to the castle and all the wealth that went with it. Only the Earl of Strathmore, his oldest normal son, the family lawyer, and the manager of the estate knew about him.

The monster was not expected to survive for very long, but he was very strong and outlived several generations of Strathmores. Each oldest son was told the awful secret when he reached the age of twenty-one.

It is said that the Strathmores were very unhappy, moody, and with-

44

drawn men because of the secret existence of their monstrous relative. It wasn't until the early twentieth century that the creature was said to have died. It is believed that his corpse is bricked up somewhere within the walls of the castle.

No one knows where the secret room is located. Once, according to Peter Underwood in his book *A Gazetteer of British Ghosts,* a group of young people visited every one of the more than one hundred rooms in Glamis Castle and hung sheets out the windows to mark them. "They were sure that they had visited every room," wrote Underwood. "But when they gathered outside they counted seven windows in the massive castle with nothing hanging from them." The mystery as to why more windows are seen from the outside than the inside remains unexplained.

The ghost of an unidentified small woman is a frequent sight in the castle chapel, even in broad daylight. The sunlight coming through the windows has been seen shining directly through the woman's figure.

Another female figure frequently appears above the clock tower, enveloped by a reddish glow. She is thought to be Janet Douglas, the wife of the sixth Lord of Glamis, who was suspected of poisoning her husband. In 1537 she was accused of trying to poison King James V and was burned at the stake.

Unusual and frightening noises are often heard within the castle walls, including stamping and swearing from the tower and hammering and loud knocking sounds. There's even a door that opens by itself every night, no matter how well locked or secured it is.

There are more than enough spirits and supernatural phenomena at Glamis Castle to impress even the most skeptical ghost watcher.

West Bengal, India

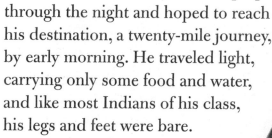

The young man had planned a surprise visit to friends and relatives in a distant village. As was the custom among those who were poor and lived in India, he began his travels after dark in order to escape the extreme heat of the day. He was prepared to walk through the night and hoped to reach his destination, a twenty-mile journey, by early morning. He traveled light, carrying only some food and water, and like most Indians of his class, his legs and feet were bare.

The road was no wider than a trail and the surface was covered by several inches of dust. Walking at a fairly brisk pace, the young man's bare foot came down directly on the coiled back of an Indian cobra snake (called the common cobra), which was lying quite comfortably and somewhat hidden from view in the warm road.

The snake reacted so quickly to what it believed to be an attack that the young man had no time to

46

respond. The six-foot-long cobra spread its frightening hood, arched its neck, and struck at the young man's legs with a sharp hissing sound.

Biting the youth's foot, it held on with its short fangs and injected a large amount of its powerful venom into the flesh. The young man screamed and tried to kick the snake away, but he knew immediately that he was doomed. In such an isolated spot there was no way to find an antivenin in time to save his life.

He screamed for help, but no one heard his cries. Within fifteen minutes of the bite, the young man's eyelids began to droop. He had difficulty swallowing and felt weak and confused. Gasping for air, his pulse became irregular. The poisonous venom was rapidly taking its toll on his nervous system and weakening his heart and lungs. Soon his system shut down completely and the young man quietly passed away, one of the fifteen thousand people who die each year in India of snakebites.

Certain districts in the Indian state of West Bengal in the Ganges River Delta report an annual death rate twice as high as that of the entire country—about eleven deaths from snakebites per one hundred thousand population. This is a frighteningly high statistic, and it may be even higher since so many villages are so isolated that they may not report incidents of snakebites.

India is a country of nearly nine hundred million people, more than three times larger than the population of the United States and crowded into an area one-third its size. This density of population coupled with the large number of dangerous Asiatic snakes in the region results in this astonishingly high death rate from snakebites.

Certain districts in West Bengal report an annual death rate from snakebites twice as high as that of the entire country of India.

Several other factors contribute to the problem as well. Most Indians seldom wear shoes or leggings to protect their feet and legs, and many travel at night when their chances of accidentally confronting a deadly snake are greater, since several lethal varieties are nocturnal species. In addition, snakes and other creatures are protected and not killed in India because many of the people believe in reincarnation, namely that the soul and spirit of a person can be reborn into an animal.

WEST BENGAL, INDIA

Housing construction among the masses is generally of poor quality, and many Indians sleep on the floor. Snakes that prowl at night are attracted to villages by the prevalence of mice and rats, which are their favorite foods. During the rainy season snakes gravitate to high ground along with people and enter homes and even beds. Sleepers are often bitten by kraits, a type of snake that is more common in populated areas and whose venom is similar to the cobra.

India is also home to the king cobra, the largest, most poisonous snake in the world. The king cobra averages eight to twelve feet in length, with the biggest on record measuring eighteen feet four inches. Imagine a snake that large and dangerous and ready to strike!

There are many unique and wondrous attractions that draw visitors to India from throughout the world, including the Taj Mahal, one of the most beautiful buildings on earth. If you're planning an Indian vacation soon, be sure to choose a pair of sturdy knee-high hiking boots. And it wouldn't hurt to bring along a snakebite kit. *Bon Voyage!*

Cheesman Park
Denver, Colorado

At first glance Cheesman Park appears to be a beautiful and pleasant place, a touch of green in the middle of a busy city. The lawns are carefully maintained and the dignified old trees provide shady spots for visitors.

Kids play here. People relax, take walks, engage in conversation, or sit and feed the squirrels and birds. Except for the Cheesman Memorial Pavilion, which is made of white marble and was built to resemble the Greek Parthenon, Cheesman Park is not much different from thousands of other parks in thousands of other American cities.

Or is it?

For beneath the well-manicured lawns and stately trees and gardens, right under the feet of the happy children and chattering adults, are the abandoned graves and forgotten bodies of dozens of Denver citizens. And you can be sure these spirits are not resting in peace! When their story is told it's not surprising that people say Cheesman Park is haunted and that ghostly apparitions are frequently reported in and around the area.

In 1858 one of Denver's founders, William Larimer, set aside this land for a town cemetery. It was first called Mount Prospect, but eventually the name was changed to City Cemetery.

By the 1880s ownership of the cemetery had passed from William Larimer to his assistant John J. Walley. By this time it was run down, badly maintained, and an embarrassing eyesore for the city. In 1890 the U.S. government assumed ownership of the land when it was discovered that it was part of an old Indian treaty. They, in turn, sold it to the city of Denver, which made plans to turn the area into a park.

City officials announced that friends and families had ninety days to relocate the bodies of their loved ones from City Cemetery. Unfortunately, five thousand of the dead remained unclaimed. These bodies were removed in 1893 by an undertaker named McGovern. The city contracted for each body to be dug up and placed in a new three-and-one-half-foot box for reburial in Denver's Riverside Cemetery.

As time passed, the workmen got progressively careless. Instead of carefully prying open the caskets, they smashed them open with shovels. Bodies that hadn't decayed enough to fit into the small coffins were broken into pieces. Body parts often were mixed up and placed in the wrong caskets.

No prayers were said for the dead, no respect given to the poor souls whose bodies were thoughtlessly shoveled into the boxes. It was around this time that residents in the area reported seeing apparitions and hearing sorrowful cries and moaning coming from the cemetery at night.

Soon the newspapers began covering the bizarre and horrible activities at the cemetery. When it was discovered that questionable financial transactions were taking place, a big scandal erupted. The project was immediately

DENVER, COLORADO

stopped and an investigation begun. The rest of the bodies were left in the cemetery. Soon they were abandoned and forgotten. Landscaping for the park began years later, and in 1907 the portion that covered City Cemetery was named after a prominent citizen of Denver, Walter Cheesman.

Some park visitors have detected a sad and disturbing undercurrent of feelings intertwined with the pleasant, happy surroundings. Perhaps it's the mournful spirits of the forsaken dead. Do they continue to search in vain for a proper burial ground where they can finally rest in peace?

The courageous person who walks down shadowy pathways of the park at night may see some interesting apparitions in the moonlight . . . if he or she doesn't run away, screaming, too quickly!

Amazon River, Brazil

"On September 19, 1981, more than 300 people were reportedly killed and eaten when an overloaded passenger-cargo boat capsized and sank as it was docking at the Brazilian port of Obidos. According to one official, only 178 of the boat's passengers survived."

—Guinness Book of Records 1994

The creatures responsible for this horrible incident were piranhas, the most ferocious freshwater fish in the world. Only two species of piranhas can inflict such terrible damage on people—the red-bellied piranhas and the black piranhas. Both types inhabit the slow-moving waters of the Amazon River in Brazil, South America.

The Amazon River is 3,900 miles long and flows through numerous freshwater channels in northern Brazil before finally draining into the Atlantic Ocean. The heavy rainfall and hot, humid weather conditions in the Amazon create an ideal environment for piranhas. During the rainy season these frightening fish thrive in the river's flood-plain, which measures nearly thirty miles across.

Piranhas grow up to fourteen inches in length and are noted for their sharp teeth and powerful jaws. The triangular-shaped upper and lower teeth slide against each other to bite off chunks of flesh, which are then swallowed whole.

Piranhas eat other fish as well as fruits, seeds, and even plants. They especially enjoy the flesh of dead animals and people. In fact, some rain-forest people use the piranhas' lethal efficiency to dispose of their dead when the river floods its banks during the rainy season. Since bodies can't be buried when there is flooding, they are left in the river. Within hours the piranhas eat all the corpses' flesh so that only the skeletons are left. The bones are then recovered, dried, and eventually buried.

AMAZON RIVER, BRAZIL

Piranhas are so thorough in eating flesh off a skeleton that it's often difficult to determine the cause of death. In the ferry-boat accident noted by the *Guinness Book of Records,* the proficiency of these deadly fish made it nearly impossible to determine the cause of death of the victims. Some may have been attacked by schools of piranhas while flailing around in the water just after the boat capsized. Others may have drowned first and then had their bodies eaten by the vicious fish.

Regardless of what may have happened, South Americans who live along the banks of the Amazon have learned to carefully coexist and even avail themselves of these frightening creatures. The flesh of piranhas is used as food, their jaws as cutting tools, and their teeth as razors. Though some may say piranhas are more useful dead than alive, they do contribute to the environment in several ways. Piranhas eat dead flesh in the river that might otherwise poison the water, and they control the fish population by eating diseased and weaker ones.

Brazil may have more than its share of beautiful sandy beaches and vacation spots, but thanks to the pesky piranhas, the Amazon River frightens away as many tourists as it attracts.

With its densely forested, lush green surroundings, the Amazon River may appear deliciously enticing, tempting you to soak those aching arches after a long day of sightseeing in the rain forest. But remember, if you dangle your feet here, you may come up a few toes shy!

Piranhas grow up to fourteen inches in length and are noted for their razor-sharp teeth and powerful jaws.

52

Interstate 65
Between Evergreen and
Greenville, Alabama

It looks like a perfectly normal stretch of road, like so many others throughout the state of Alabama.

In official reports the police refer to it as "open country." Others say it's a lonely and isolated stretch through forested land. A few go so far as to describe it as "spooky" and "haunted."

One thing is definite, though. Something strange and scary is happening on Interstate 65 between the small towns of Evergreen and Greenville, and even the police can't explain it! The facts clearly show that the number of accidents on this forty-mile stretch of I-65 is considerably higher than average. And the big mystery is why?

Judge for yourself: In the time period from 1987 through mid-October of 1994, there have been 724 accidents recorded. According to statistics supplied by Waymon Benifield of the Alabama Department of Transportation in Montgomery, 989 vehicles were involved in these accidents, nearly 400 people were injured, and 31 were killed.

Some say it's just a coincidence. County Sheriff Edwin Booker once declared that "drivers simply lose interest." Were they so hypnotized by the straight and flat terrain that they lost their concentration, as the police seem to think? But the country is full of straight, flat roads whose accident statistics are nowhere near the high figures of Interstate 65 between Evergreen and Greenville, Alabama!

There's talk in the area that this portion of the highway was constructed over sacred Creek Indian burial grounds. Many locals believe that the spirits of the Indians, whose graves were disturbed, are exerting some kind of power over the drivers.

Are drivers swerving to avoid visions of ghosts or other apparitions that appear out of nowhere on the highway? Are angry spirits causing drivers to lapse into a trancelike state and lose control of their cars?

Tribal Chairman Eddie Tullis of the local Creek Indian reservation stated, "A lot of our people's graves were disturbed by the interstate," but he stopped short of blaming Indian spirits for the accidents. "I think if people consider how the Indians have been mistreated," said Tullis in *More Haunted Houses* by Joan Bingham and Delores Riccio, "it could cause them to lose their attention while on the road."

INTERSTATE 65, ALABAMA

One might expect an increase in accidents in the winter months at night when the weather was bad and visibility limited. Yet the data clearly shows that over 60 percent of the accidents took place in the daylight hours, when it was clear or cloudy and the roads were dry, not wet, icy, or snowy.

Surprisingly most accidents occurred in the summer months on straight level stretches where the driver's vision was not obstructed in any way. Most drivers were wide awake, alert, and paying attention.

It's even more mysterious when you consider that the majority of the accidents involved only one vehicle!

Has a large amount of hostile energy built up in this area? Apparently so. In addition to having their sacred burial grounds disturbed, the Creek Indians were forced by the Federal government in the 1830s to leave their homes in Alabama and resettle on reservations in Oklahoma. According to Bingham and Riccio, thousands died in the migration west.

No one really knows what's causing the high number of accidents on that portion of the Interstate in southern Alabama. But one thing is certain. If you find yourself driving there one day, keep awake, stay alert, and be very, very careful—no matter how beautiful the day may seem!

Mammoth and Crystal Caves, Mammoth Cave National Park, Kentucky

Joy Lyons, a guide at Mammoth Cave, had just led a group of tourists along with two other park rangers to a place in the big cave called the Church. Here the guides turned off the lights so the tourists could "have a sensory experience."

Suddenly Lyons was shoved hard on the right shoulder so forcefully that she almost toppled over. At that exact instant one of the rangers lit a lantern and Lyons saw, to her amazement, that no one else in the cave was even remotely close to where she was standing.

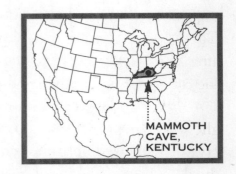

MAMMOTH CAVE, KENTUCKY

Who pushed her? Was it one of the several ghosts and apparitions that have appeared out of nowhere to dozens of visitors and guides, only to disappear just as fast? Or was it just Lyons' imagination playing tricks on her?

Arthur Myers in his book *A Ghosthunter's Guide* interviewed numerous people who have experienced strange and unexplained phenomena in both Mammoth Cave and Crystal Cave (two attractions in Mammoth Cave National Park), and Joy Lyons was just one of them.

Even without the possibility of ghosts, Mammoth Cave's underground caverns and passageways are frightening enough. It's certainly a place where one would rather not be left alone. Becky Dahle, a supervisor of the attraction's guides, told Myers, "If there ever was a place under the earth where people's imaginations could play tricks on them, it's Mammoth Cave. It's a deprivational thing," she explained. "There's no natural light, no natural sound." In other words, it's pretty creepy.

Mammoth Cave is the largest cave in the world, estimated to be about 340 million years old. It's easy to get hopelessly lost here, since there are 330 miles of passageways on five different levels. A mummified body of an Indian man, more than two thousand years old, has been found here along with other evidence of early human habitation.

Many guides and tourists have had strange experiences. One believed he saw the ghost of a famous guide from the nineteenth century named Stephen Bishop, a former slave who always wore a large Panama hat. Several have seen a man in old-fashioned dress standing apart from the main group of tourists.

Crystal Cave, located five miles from Mammoth Cave, is known for the bizarre death of its one-time owner, Floyd Collins, in 1925. He became trapped under a rock overhang and for sixteen days rescue attempts to free Collins were reported in newspapers throughout the country. He died after an unexpected cave-in, and his glass-topped coffin was displayed in the cave as a tourist attraction for a number of years.

Many strange occurrences at Crystal Cave have been linked to the ghost of Floyd Collins. One employee distinctly heard a man's voice faintly crying, "Help! Help me, Johnny, I'm trapped!" It's interesting to note that the last person to talk with Floyd Collins before the cave-in was his friend Johnny Gerald!

People's voices in conversation, candles flaming up for no apparent reason, sounds of rhythmic banging, flapping noises like the wings of birds, an ancient crank-up telephone that's disconnected but suddenly rings—all of these were experienced at Crystal Cave by a variety of people.

Are there ghosts in Mammoth Cave and Crystal Cave?

According to author Myers, "If there aren't, a lot of people are hallucinating."

Suicide Pool
Epping Forest, England

Early one morning in the summer of 1914 a man was taking a walk on one of the many hiking trails in Epping Forest, ten miles northeast of the city of London. As he neared a body of water popularly known as the Suicide Pool, he noticed the figure of a man lying facedown in a ditch. Another man, overweight and stocky, was standing over the apparently dead body with a gun still clutched in his hand.

EPPING FOREST, ENGLAND

Impulsively the man approached the armed man to question him. Before he could get a single word out of his mouth, however, both the man with the gun and the body in the ditch disappeared right before his eyes.

Did the man imagine the bizarre scene? No one knows for sure.

Two days later the body of a former soldier was found lying facedown in the same ditch. The poor man had clearly died from gunshot wounds, and the police listed his death as a homicide. The murderer was never caught, and the man's death remains one of the many strange mysteries that surround the Suicide Pool and its vicinity in Epping Forest.

According to Elliott O'Donnell in his book *The Great Ghost Hunter*, "There is no pool of water in England which has been the scene of more suicides and murders and . . . which is more sinister in reputation . . . "

One of Europe's oldest forests, Epping is a six-thousand-acre maze of hiking paths and horsetrails crisscrossed by roadways. Legislation passed in 1878 established a portion of the forest to be preserved for recreational activities. Formally opened to the public by Queen Victoria in 1882,

Epping Forest is located near the towns of Woodford and Waltham and is easily accessible to Londoners by railway.

Surrounded by trees, the Suicide Pool is a dark and still body of water. A number of murders have been associated with the area but one of the better-known cases is the unsolved mystery of a pretty young servant named Emma Morgan. She was last seen alive walking toward Epping Forest with a baby in her arms. Morgan's husband had thrown her and her child out of the house when he discovered the baby wasn't his.

On that particular day Emma Morgan and her child were not only homeless, but penniless as well. It's possible she may have been heading to the Suicide Pool to end her misery, but the woman never made it. The bodies of Morgan and her baby were found brutally murdered next to the water. The killer was never found.

Author O'Donnell visited the Suicide Pool one moonlit autumn night and had several frightening experiences. Although totally alone, he distinctly heard someone cough, the faint cry of a child in pain, and then the sounds of a group of people steadily marching toward the pool. When the tramping sounds stopped, O'Donnell clearly saw several black-robed figures holding a coffin. Hearing a noise from the opposite direction, he turned and saw an image of an "evil-looking" young man bending over the body of a woman. According to O'Donnell, "Picking up the body, he came staggering with it to the pool and threw the body into the still, gleaming water." Then the images faded and all was quiet again.

O'Donnell described his strange experience to an older man who had lived near Epping Forest for many years. The man brought out old newspaper clippings that described the unsolved case of a woman who had been murdered and thrown into the Suicide Pool in 1887.

Is the area around the Suicide Pool so imprinted with tragedy and bloodshed that certain sensitive individuals experience violent replays of the past and terrible visions of the future?

O'Donnell thought so. What do you think?

Alcatraz
San Francisco, California

Walking down the now-vacant corridors of what once was the U.S. Penitentiary at Alcatraz, one finds the cell doors propped open, one after the other, leading into empty, stark cubicles. A strange and eerie timelessness hovers in the air here, as if the past were permanently imprisoned within the same walls where so many convicts were once locked behind bars.

What's that? A clang of metal doors, the sound of men's voices? Turning around quickly, you see there is nothing there—only emptiness. Yet some security guards and tour guides have reported hearing similar sounds here—screaming, whistling, even the sound of feet running along the corridors.

For nearly thirty years the U.S. Penitentiary at Alcatraz was a place of violence, brutality, and loneliness. Now a national park and popular tourist attraction, it is not at all surprising that this once harsh and dismal place is said to be haunted by the frightening sounds of the past.

First used as a fortress to protect San Francisco Bay during Civil War days, the rocky island became a military prison in 1861. By the 1920s stories circulated concerning the severity of life at Alcatraz. One San Francisco newspaper reporter called it "Uncle Sam's Devil's Island,"

comparing it to the famous penal colony of Devil's Island off French Guiana in the Caribbean Sea.

In 1933 the Department of Justice acquired the island, and on July 1, 1934, Alcatraz became a U.S. penitentiary. It was converted to a maximum security prison in response to the nationwide crime wave of the 1930s. Only dangerous, difficult, and desperate inmates were sent here to serve "hard time." They were murderers, rapists, and gangsters and included the likes of Al Capone and Machine Gun Kelly.

Surrounded by San Francisco Bay, "the rock" seemed virtually impossible to escape from. Yet there were eight escape attempts from Alcatraz. Five were stopped by bullets, and the others were presumed drowned in the frigid waters of the Bay. On May 2, 1946, six inmates attempted to break out by capturing several guards. In the gun battle that followed, three of the inmates and two of the guards were killed and several others were wounded.

Surrounded by San Francisco Bay, "the rock" was virtually impossible to escape from.

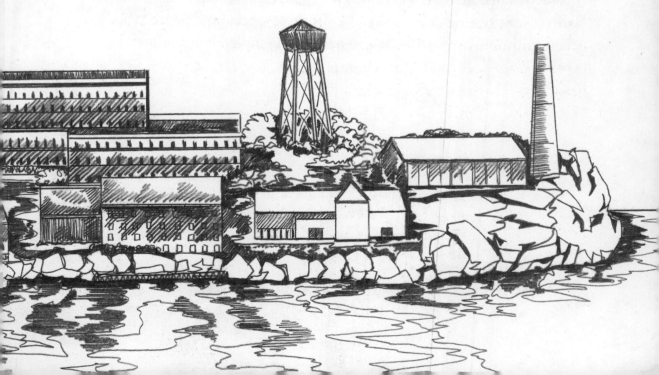

The most famous break occurred on June 11, 1962, when Frank Lee Morris, Clarence Anglin, and John Anglin chipped out a tunnel through concrete and then used the prison ventilation system to escape from the cellhouse. They made their way to the water and were never heard from again. To this day it's uncertain whether the men drowned or actually escaped to the mainland.

According to Rosemary Ellen Guiley in *The Encyclopedia of Ghosts and Spirits,* "Insanity was the kindest fate to befall a prisoner—others committed suicide, murdered one another, or died unpleasant deaths from illness and disease. Beatings by guards were routine," wrote Guiley, "and the screams of the beaten reverberated throughout the cells."

The worst conditions at Alcatraz were found in solitary confinement cells in Block D (called "holes" by the inmates) where many men either became very ill, went insane, or died. A prisoner was stripped naked, beaten, and kept in complete darkness in a tiny cement cell with only a hole in the floor for a bathroom. Bread and water were fed to the prisoners twice a day and every third day they were given a full meal.

Do the sounds of a violent past replay themselves over and over again in the empty corridors of Alcatraz? Are these sounds just the result of an overactive imagination stimulated by such a strange and scary setting? Perhaps. But some believe that the death, savagery, and horror that took place within the prison walls can never be completely erased.

Bachelor's Grove Cemetery, Rubio Woods Chicago, Illinois

The dead don't rest easy at Bachelor's Grove Cemetery! How else could you explain the reports of strange lights, unusual cold, ghostly apparitions, phantom cars, and spirit voices?

It's no wonder that this cemetery is considered by many to be one of the most haunted in the world. Dale Kaczmarek, head of the Ghost Research Society, has documented the scary and mysterious phenomena that have occurred here over the years.

Consider the following:

- One woman reported colliding with a car at a nearby intersection. When she got out to inspect her front fender, the other car had disappeared and there was absolutely no damage to her vehicle.

CHICAGO, ILLINOIS

- There have been numerous reports of a phantom red skyrocket zooming above the main path leading to the cemetery, leaving a red trail behind it. And some of these lights, according to Kaczmarek, "have been seen in broad daylight"!
- Many visitors to the cemetery have seen the apparitions of a woman carrying a baby, a dark-hooded figure, and a mysterious black carriage.

In addition, a number of people have observed a phantom farmhouse that appears and then vanishes without a trace. Whether it's in daylight or evening, "the description of the house," explained Kaczmarek, "remains constant: a white farmhouse with white wooden pillars, a porch swing, and a light burning faintly in the window."

He continued, "As the house is approached by witnesses, it begins to shrink and get smaller and smaller until the image itself disappears from sight. No one has ever made it to the front steps. . . . " he added. Could the farmhouse be the entrance to another dimension?

German immigrants originally settled in the area in the 1830s, which was given its name because of the large number of unmarried men living there. One acre of land was set aside for the graveyard, and burials continued there until 1965. The cemetery is surrounded by an eight-foot-high fence riddled by holes. The main gates are broken and everything is overgrown with weeds and other foliage.

Inside, the gravestones have been vandalized, moved, and marked with graffiti and spray paint. According to Kaczmarek, during the 1920s and 1930s gangsters used the lagoon to dump dead bodies. In 1964 and 1975 some graves were dug up and caskets broken into. In the middle 1970s rangers found evidence of voodoo and devil worship. Could the dark-hooded figure have some connection to this black magic?

It's interesting to note that within the fence bordering the cemetery there are no squirrels, birds, chipmunks, or other animals. "It is literally devoid of life," explained Kaczmarek. Yet, just outside the fence, plenty of these animals can been seen and heard in the Rubio Woods. Do the animals sense that all is not right at Bachelor's Grove? Are the troubled spirits unhappy because their final resting places have been disturbed and violated? No one knows.

The animals have decided to stay away. But many curious people still continue to find the courage to investigate this scary and haunted place.

Will you be one of them?